SLIP

SLIP

POEMS BY SINA QUEYRAS

MISFIT   ECW PRESS

NATIONAL LIBRARY OF CANADA CATALOGUING IN PUBLICATION DATA

Queyras, Sina, 1963–
Slip

Poems.
ISBN 1-55022-479-4

I. Title.

PS8583.U341485 2001   C811'.6   C2001-900816-3
PR9199.4.Q4985 2001

Edited by Michael Holmes / a misFit book
Cover and text design by Tania Craan
Cover art by Christine Willcox
Layout by Mary Bowness

Printed by AGMV

Distributed in Canada by
General Distribution Services,
325 Humber College Blvd.,
Toronto, ON M9W 7C3

Published by ECW PRESS
2120 Queen Street East, Suite 200
Toronto, ON M4E 1E2
ecwpress.com

This book is set in Garamond.

PRINTED AND BOUND IN CANADA

The publication of *Slip* has been generously supported by the Canada Council,
the Ontario Arts Council and the Government of Canada through the Book
Publishing Industry Development Program. Canadä

Without warning

As a whirlwind
swoops on an oak
Love shakes my heart
— Sappho

Remind me of what's coming, not what's past.
— Marilyn Hacker

I

SCRABBLING

1.

Apartment-hunting the plateau: dancer, painter, cellist,
two engineers (Good God!), and an over-ripe woman

with pears for teeth who offered a smoke, borrowed a dollar
in return. No decisions yet. One pleasant surprise: Marg's

midnight call. All's well, though TO's all flash and straw,
talk of screenwriting-slash-money, leave poetry behind.

We are neither of us career poets, she says, slipping
your number in. I leave it floating in the still-warm breeze

to let the winds of fate decide. Harmless, harmless, I sing
myself to sleep, and yet I cannot say your name.

2.

Wake to the sun. Chaton mauling a sparrow on the porch
next door where the women fuck so descriptively I want to yell

Doucement, ma clitoris! But where does the accent fall? *La
langue française* eludes me even more than English,

and who can I ask? The women rarely come up for air,
and Sylv crafts harnesses and whips of leather: *I'll fit you*

one! (Mon Dieu.) Who can I tell I've not even seen
the apparatus, never mind one harnessed between my thighs?

Just two days, already my innocence is threatened, my
island fades. Fickle self: apartment-hunting the plateau,

my heart with L., who knows where my head is, my
body's desire a mystery to me.

3.

Elbows cold on marble: third day of September
and already the air bristles. Despite myself, I slip

a quarter into the phone, and before this bowl of café
au lait empties, you'll sit eye to eye no place to hide.

Will I recognize your eyes, your eyes mine? Your words,
will they explode my ears or melt like chocolate

on my tongue? Not yet here, I'm thinking tongue, thinking
fingers running through hair, thinking aubergine! Too

delicious. I will not sip my coffee, will not move my hands,
will not look up, but then the sun arrives, morning glory

unfolds its silk: a powdery trembling as the door swings
open wide my heart.

4.

The door swings wide and Scrabble game in hand
you've come to conquer — but this is my *forté*

my lascivious grad school girl. Don't fret, I'll leave
no teeth marks on your neck: I can't sink in. A wife

I have and am. We have a life. But too soon
this false bravado fades, my sad resolve as senseless

as the shopkeeper's *Bienvenue!* If I could keep my eyes
on your mouth (your mouth!) and not your ear,

your chin, the line that draws me to the cleave
of your blue blouse, I might have half a chance.

But no, the beaded strings, earrings, the timbre
of your laugh and I'm cast off, adrift. I float down

the Main, glass baubles bobbing over espresso waves.

5.

And why resolve? In this the autumn of my thirty-first
year, I'm half a continent from home — living single —

for the first, possibly last, time in my life. A student
in Leonard Cohen's town, on stone-laid avenues,

reading poems in cafés and bars: flirt — how could I not?
You talk Toronto for High Holidays. How harmless.

(I'm listening, yes, trying not to imagine you there.)
Finally you lay out the game, an upturned boat,

my nostrils tingling with you, sneezing, you offer
me tissue, offer me coffee, offer me your laugh.

Impossible! How do you know exactly what I lack?
Reach out so easily, so instinctively — the way your elbow

rests in the strut of your flattened hand: your fingertips
undo me.

6.

Got to remember who I am. Remember cabin, garden,
chickens, how I loved naked-walking to the bathhouse,

how even in winter I kept the door open, and from
the steaming tub hoped to catch a grazing doe.

I tell you of my pining, but it's more reminder than
I can admit. At least in this moment, the sun,

the Main, the calzone, the café — there's nowhere else.
But look at you. Not yet thirty, this is just a game.

Level-headed you'll return to the family way, marry
a doctor, lawyer, propagate, worship your career,

travel once a year someplace safe, and remember me
(fondly?) from your untamed student days.

7.

I've Scrabbled since the age of six, trusting, I'm willing
to spell words long before meaning. Tile by tile

I am betrayed, bead, seam, blouse, hand, skin; word
by word my undoing for anyone to read. We sit

in the window of the Euro-deli, marble table cool,
clowns on stilts, street performers, children screaming,

discordant harmonica gypsy music. The details insist
themselves: two dykes from L'Androgyne, tongues in each

other's mouths, Christoph with his green cap, the scent
of apples, maple leaves turning, and two dogs tied

to a meter outside do not stop whining.

8.

You invite me for dinner, a party to follow. Swollen-tongued,
I nod my acceptance, a waft of chlorine filling my nose, metal

rungs extremely slippery. No handrail, suddenly my brow,
my breast wet. Suddenly a belly flop of sky, and dizzy:

there's your hand again. Did anyone notice how close our
knees are? Did the light turn apricot to emphasize your eyes?

Are you a plot against my past, colour and curl designed
to entice me from my path? The questions logjam:

Is your hair heavy? How do you comb it? Were you born
with it like that? Do people touch it on the street? Does it

cushion your head at night? Does it shape your dreams? How
do you sleep? Or, more precisely, will you sleep with me?

9.

If I slip now
If my tongue is brash
If my thoughts betray
If my feet numb
If I fall
If my tongue
If the shell cracks
If our knees touch
If words fail
If our eyes meet
If my heart softens
If the sun
If tongue
If word
If numb
If heart skin tongue word embrace

Fall

I will deny it all

10.

Is it possible to sip coffee and play Scrabble while
plotting seduction, alibis, alternate realities,

and still find time to compose a line or two?
Your hand across the table a fist in a balloon,

the tension surprises even you. What portrait might
I paint? Botticelli at Clayoquot? The Venus emerging

from a four-hundred-year-old fir? Mona Lisa
meets Courtney Love? For now my tongue

is abalone, my heart the flattened roadside boot,
the one glove in the metro, my mind Berri station,

I have ten seconds to decide, I'm mourning
a journey gone deliciously off course, or on.

11.

My throbbing head! This may not be the first game I've tied,
but it is the first game I've played so completely. You

circle our scores, matter-of-factly slip the paper into
the box and with it (I hope) a seed of me. It will take little

prodding to make me grow, and on (or at or during) Rosh
Hashanah, this salacious Romeo — your heart held high

in my triumphant hand — out of your Scrabble bag will
rise. Head afloat, I bounce along beside you to the corner

of Prince Arthur because there is nowhere else to go.

II

UNCONSCIOUS COURTSHIP

There's a strange frenzy in my head,
of birds flying,
each particle circulating on its own.
Is the one I love everywhere?
— Rumi

AVENUE LAVAL

Flush with possibilities I move in to the basement suite in your brick
building, the only red on a block of lavish greystones trimmed in chalky
greens and Madame Caillaud in her wool suit welcomes me to the tiny
anglo fold. I tell myself it's because you're near that I wander up
to your flat; I tell myself it's because of Montreal that we lie
on your bed eating plum tomatoes; I tell myself it's because of Foucault
that I can't sleep; I tell myself I'm not falling in love, and yet late nights
reading Ginsberg until our tongues are tied in his long breathless lines.

OWLY I AM

Letters from home come filled with details: *the chickens are scratching,*
I'm opening a beer, I had a fire last night. I sit in the L'Anecdote, west
coast drowning out the grill, the patois: *an owl made me think of calling*
you, can't sleep, the stove burns too hot without you here, the cat restless,
leaves mice on your chair, in your shoe . . . maybe I'll mail them? It's not
too late: this island, my lion, a diversion yet and full of hope I kiss
the envelope. So many details left out. In just eight weeks I'll be back
to you my most devoted one. And you? That makes two yous, one me:
my heart threatens to split
not so neatly in two.

VERMONT, DRIVING

Annie and I in her blue Sunbird, fall a Motown breeze. We praise
the divas through brick and steepled towns all Gap and Americana.
Garcia cones from Ben and Jerry's, we search the golden streets
for Larry, Darryl and Darryl. (Of course she loves Newhart
too.) We belly-laughed and spoke (illicitly) of you (my love?). She
calls me Piglet because I'm cautious but brave. She's Pooh
of course, and you, a perfect Eeyore. I know you'll not be amused,
but there is something donkey about your mien
and solemn eyes.

INSOMNIA 1

Another midnight coastal call. Guilt-heavy my head hangs for what
I have not yet done: even as I'm out the door, her eyes. They've turned
the fountain off in Carré Saint-Louis, *des érables flambés*. Soon
a thin ice path where the sidewalk is. One foot in the garden, one foot
on ice, this tightrope walking has my perspective askew. Fall asleep,
wake up, fall asleep — with visions of whom I cannot say. But tonight
Virginia wading through snow, a slim volume (the novels even more
distilled) in hand, her eyes lighthouse beams, she says, *How can you be
in two beds at once? Slice the ties! Slice!*

INSOMNIA 2

Three nights, no sleep, my mind is playing tricks on me: this morning
Virginia on the pool bottom in mountain pose. Toured the old port,
Mont-Royal, parc La Fontaine, and still wide awake. It's midnight and
we're off to Club Sky on St-Catherine — I'll dance with kittens, tire
myself that way. But it's my slim-hipped girl who makes me want
to come. Her lasso is *formidable:* can barely duck the swings
these days, fling myself in front of her shamelessly. The wind tickles
my lips. This is no way to transcend desire. I slip suit jacket over
camisole: I need cool air, and something soft to touch my skin, if not
her hand.

BISTRO QUATRE

A cabernet with Lyell while outside two women in evening gown,
and tux, serenade the sun's decline with flute and viola.
I can't help searching for Gail Scott in the corner booth — I'm sure
I'd know her face. But here and now, Lyell across from me, spends
his last days projecting other people's art, so angry, the HIV
much more than a hooked metaphor coursing through his veins.
The worst is how your friends all fall away, he says. *When Patrick
died I called each number in his book, and no one came. I hold them
in my arms, and I'm alone again.* It isn't fair, all this dying
in one another's arms. If I could hold him in my arms and let him
cry. If I could hold him. If he would cry.

EVERYTHING SEEMS SO BLAND

Cappuccino Commotion for Seinfeld tonight. Happy you're here squeezing
Barthes and Kristeva between spoonfuls and punch lines, happy you're
laughing, happy to corrupt your palate with sitcoms. Trying not to imagine
how you'll refine mine, not to calculate the cost of opening myself, not
to notice how easily my hand strays and how each time you sit closer,
how each time we laugh I feel another layer strip, want to control, contain,
constrict, keep this textual — while what I wept to leave weeks ago —
grows faint.

THE GREY CAT

Arrives between snowfalls,
sashays through my open door,
his tail curling once round
each leg, without a sniff
tiptoes to the futon, curls
on my Woody Woodpecker
sheets his eyes blinking
once, twice, three times before
he sleeps, and it occurs
to me this may be home.

DOWN THE RIVER, MADLY

Drinking Maudite, lighting du Mauriers off the butts, describing every
nuance of your body, recounting every word you've said, discussing
at length each interpretation, translating the smell of you, the inspiration
of you, the talk and walking to school of you, until Billy asks when I'll kiss
you and I insist that my interest is innocent, I haven't imagined your lips
on mine, and yes, we're going out tomorrow night, and yes I'll be your
date, but it's not how it looks at all. Billy says the current is strong —
if I need a life preserver, I know who to call.

FOUR STEPS

1.

Woke in a sweat, tears, longing, hung over, maudlin.
Repentant I will escort you, in due course return unmoved

to my camping futon, the grey cat sleeping there.
Footfalls overhead: from desk to bed each move

a lightening bolt, and lust-stung, benumbed — I cannot
leave my bed. My doubled-heart a throbbing, open sore

and tears for wanting what I cannot, in good faith, have.
It's fun, L. says, *you need to have.* And if my diversions

are not alone, my longest lasting love? Some questions
better left unasked.

2.

Pumpkin sky. Breathless I beat up the stairs and buzz.
Your flat an autumn pond: tacit, silken, I launch into

the layers of your blouse, your skirt, the length
of your legs — I have not yet seen the muscle of them.

You hook earrings dangled in steely light, and I'm
a speckled trout, a morsel for your enormous

appetite, content to dangle or drown with you tonight.
We stop, pick up another bottle of Gato Negro and, laughing,

you ask me to see you home: I say I might.

3.

The party ten years too young: no distractions here.
And though you stalked the room — gaze a lion's mane

upon my neck — cigarettes lit, glasses drained, all night,
even as Rabbit passed out, and Pooh needed help with her

to bed; through a gnarl of safety-pinned girls, leggings torn
and pastel hair; of sweatered preppy boys, earnest, career-

minded, professorial rumouring over the too loud music,
anywhere you moved your eyes warm and tethered. Would

we be quite the same in just three years time? Or, having
vaulted flaming hurdles, climax and decline.

4.

Arm-in-arm we stagger from the metro under a star-filled,
half moon-sky, your lips, surprising as snow in June; but

this is Montreal, where sun can shine through rain
and wine can be delivered to your door.

Somewhere on Sherbrooke we bump against a brick wall,
and on Prince Arthur I lay my coat and sip by sip,

share my last beer lip to lip. I do not remember crossing
the threshold of your door, cannot imagine what I told

myself, but the grey of your eyes, smooth pebbles, pier,
August, running, naked, dive. I ask you should I be here,

now, and you say, yes, you say just kiss, your hand
on the back of my neck. No words. Nothing more to say.

IN THE NIGHT, SUDDENLY

1.

It is 6 am when I open my eyes in your bed. When you turn,
open your eyes, every muscle and vein in me expands.

If I open my mouth you will see my heart beating, how
lost I am; you pull my head to your chest. I tell myself

this is only one night, I have an island to return to. Later
in my basement room, my nose full of you, cat scent,

where your tongue has touched I glow. I'll lie here contained
in the sonatas while you lick your fur and purr

your possession of me. Already you have touched me
more than anyone, ever, everywhere. Prodigy. Beethoven

tongue.

2.

All day I feel your breath in the rub of my collar, on
my cheek and jaw where I expect your downy fingers still.

I long to kiss everyone on St-Laurent, to buy every flower,
every fruit, every book, every chocolate, and lay them

at your feet. Impossible behaviour: the cashier at
Warshaw's clucks her tongue, but I feel only Lust

with a capital L, and what is lust but the transformation
of obstacles to winged things, adoration of ascent,

muscled haunches overhead. O, the first time I've
gazed outside myself in months! There'll be no talk

of sin now, and to celebrate, new lipstick, a glass
of St-Emilion, a tomato flown from Provence to

the palm of my hand.

3.

In the reading room I feed you slices of papaya, painful
to lick the juice from your chin and not follow the line

drawing me down. How can I survive this untransformed?
Why describe desire when I can reach out to you? And

who cares about other people? My hands seek your hips,
lips, ribs, the half-shell of your underarm. What I need is:

a phone call from L., a crack in the ice, two mating
elephants, my hands in earth, seven popped balloons,

my Visa bill, reservations on the space shuttle, a trip
to Roswell, night shift at a shelter, to hear Sylvia Plath

laugh.

4.

What Cixous has to say about *jouissance* makes sense
in the flash of skin, your legs when your toes scrape

the full moon, a whole ocean pulling at my tongue. But
outside of thighs I have nothing to say. Impossible

to concentrate on the reading. When you caress your pen
I feel your fingers on my thigh and when I moan finally,

it's not because the presentation has moved me.
What do I know of Margaret Cavendish? That she did not

have the pleasure of your mouth on the inside of her elbow.
And I won't disagree that women invented the novel since

poems may not be large enough to contain them. When
you raise your hand to move a curl from your mouth I cannot

contain myself.

5.

The phone's pierce and crackle. My spine, my sunflower head
droop, shoulderless. This is the last time we will sleep together.

Just one more time is all. Each time you slip into my bed
it is the last time I will see your elbows lift; you slowly remove

your blouse. Let the arms linger, let me take in every hair
and mole, burn — the texture of you will become my tongue.

What I say when you sleep: this is another island,
in the St. Lawrence, between St-Laurent and St-Denis,

an oasis, each kiss a granule of sand underfoot or
this can't go on, can't be spoken of, and I would stay

on my knees
all night.

III

FLASH FROZEN

BOULEVARD ST-LAURENT

Knee-deep in fresh snow we make our way to the Quatre Frères
for red peppers and zucchini. Already I have accumulated layers
around the thigh and stomach, and what feels like a thousand
pounds of guilt I carry in the small of my back. Still, a snowflake
landing on chenille tingles me, expectant. Here on St-Laurent
the dendrites cut out on warm, wet, west coast afternoons
suddenly make sense. You tell me it won't last — not even Halloween
and snow falling. I want to capture a flake, mail it home: look
at the detail, look at the precision, look at the polished, still-
sharp edges. In your bed everything tastes like summer, and
with Camembert, baguette, and sunlight filling your room
there is only the presence of wool to signify October, winter,
Quebec.

NOTE BENE

Even with the flu I can't resist you. Too weak to eat, move, read, yet
your skin needs to be licked and my hand can be found much
the same way it finds you. After the arc of your back, the tremble
of your lips, you plunge into your green jeans, promise ginger ale,
promise to return for another round but the depth of your hunger
stirs me. Some people need chicken soup, for me it is breast
and thigh, O my, a morsel of Brossard, dash of Mouré — after all
this is Montréal. I'm sure the librarian has found traces of you
around my mouth. I'm sure Madame Caillaud has heard us. I'm sure
Monsieur le sexologue has been taking copious, coping, coupling, notes.
Note bene: she tastes fabulous.

AFTER A WEEKEND IN TORONTO

I come upstairs once more to tell you we're over. Press
you against the kitchen counter, kiss your neck, my
hands against the braid of your sweater, your jeans
so tight, your jeans so tight, your jeans so tight there is
no need
to touch skin.

6 DAYS IN PURGATORY

1.

I'm a hollow trunk. A home fit for a woodpecker. Soon I'll crumble
and on my back fungus and lichen will grow. Billy was right:
those who stand on moral high ground have far to fall. I've
stood too tall, too long, and L. — to whom I've promised truth
above all else — has less forgiveness than myself. If she would only
ask, I'm ready to tell. But let it wait until we're face to face, I dread
the receiver's click. Billy says honesty is foolish where distance
is concerned: no use coming clean to muddy future waters
and besides, my brave bed mate wants only a tumble to flavour
her student days. Why risk well-laid plans to become a footnote
in some future professor's imagined memoirs?

2.

Morning is too delicious in her green duvet. I'll enjoy
her mouth on mine, anchor here awhile. She holds
memory at bay. There is no trauma in her eyes, a cool
soothing gaze: cat on a porch, honeysuckle, shade. Though
if I relax, I fear she'll pounce, tear in, drag me — her spoils —
back to her lair, and my soft-shelled self defenseless
in her grip. Hours stretch themselves to days. In her
bed I'm sworn to stay, and let the bustling world away.

3.

On the up-escalator at the metro, a simple trip and Annie's ankle
snapped. It seemed benign, not even a fall, no scrapes at all. Looks
are deceiving: bear-like Annie fractures so easily and a piglet
like me tumbles (knock on wood, knock on metal, knock
on the frosted windows of my house) and nothing breaks.
Guilty (again), at the empty hospital with blue movies in the waiting
room: *How did the accident occur?* The attendant, bored; while
on TV above his head a man takes two women from behind. *Alcohol?*
Yes, we had imbibed a bottle (or two) of too-cheap dépanneur wine
while assembling Kinder toys. Though the snow fell until
the streets were drifts, unsafe to navigate, I had to see you
before the clock struck twelve, and so we wound our wool scarves,
donned our caps and now Annie all laid up and high on codeine.
(I cannot leave her side, you understand?)

4.

Dear France,

Your hair looks thick and straight, the bits of grey are good, and
I agree almost any option beats chemotherapy. I'll be home soon.
Yes, you're right, there is a "little something" in my voice. But
what has me soaring has me wallowing too. Perhaps at Christmas
we can talk while hiking your trail up Cypress Bowl. The photo
of the sisters is divine. Is it you and me framed in your window
there? Can't wait to see your flying one-breasted women (can't wait
to see you fly!). I'm writing of the novel's birth, but no passion there
and letters arrive so sad they're a two-by-four across the chest,
though at this distance what can I do? I know the west coast is not
going anywhere — it's me it seems, who has trouble staying there.

5.

Chère Billy,

Why don't you give us a chance? What us? *This.* And she kissed me
right in front of *le Musée des beaux-arts.* (We had seen the Tansey
show — you would approve.) There is no us. (*Derrida Queries de Man*
waltzing on a cliff.) *There is.* (A *Doubting Thomas.*) There's not! I turned,
she turned me back. (Everything monochrome.) What happened
to a one-night stand? (Suppressing the urge to laugh.) *One-night
stands don't linger on for weeks.* You've tricked me. (Displacement.)
No, she said, *you tricked yourself.* (Failure of representation.) I'm leaving.
(Climbing the printed word.) *You've said that many times.* I mean it (Or
diving), Wednesday afternoon. (Specificity.) *Leave? Not tell?* (Impact.) I'm
telling you now. *It's now or never. I won't be strung along this way.*
(Fumbling for a key.) I'll never love you. (Rupture.)
She held out her gloved hand and I turned my back.

I hear she's going to Italy for Christmas break.

6.

Flight details made, plans set, there is a pause so lengthy
I hear a crow calling over the hollow. *Are you having an affair?*
The question dropped, the plunk of it rippling across the worn
weave of who we were. The fallout begins: flights cancelled, offers
rescinded, the weight of it sinking and sinking until the phone
is slammed. I count the seconds before L. begins smashing
my things (Virgin Mary, snow globe, camera) random, immediate.
Pick up and dial. Pick up and dial again. All night, even as
she paces her cage above, falling on her bed, sobbing, tossing
the lilies I bought her out in the snow, busy signal, dial, busy
signal — but there is no line.

IV

SCENIC ART

DEAR SYLV,

Toronto latte, trying not to think of the west, and now, Montréal.
How did the geography of our lives become so complex? I want
to let the past dissolve before the future takes shape. I know,
I know, you have a lover in every club, but I'm not built that way.
Sorry to hear about the baths, sorry I called you slut, sorry I don't
understand public sex, with strangers, two at a time, while tied up,
whipped, lathered with oil. *Give it time, give it time,* so you say, but
mere imaginings make me wince. Of course you're right, to each
her own — so why laugh at the romantic I am? And no, I haven't
seen her. I know you hate the Euro-deli, but when you pass it,
will you look for curls?

SUBTERRANEAN

Mid-town Marg, trying on filmy
and slick dyke, her basement
on Dovercourt, a Matisse
of big-thighed women,
paper, stars, rock
around the clawfoot tub smelling
of fermenting grapes
and vanilla-scented candles.
Transformed Marg lovely
in her still-poetic skin
shaking the big-smoke
in one hand, full of Mosto
Vino and intention, but I don't
fit in this world, bang
my head on the clouds
again and again.

THE BEACHES

From Kew Beach to the sleek lines
of the filtration plant I expect to see nuns
falling through the air, handmaids gliding
across the grass, Caravaggio rising
like Venus up onto the beach, shaking
his head, his long hair, languid words
pearling.

TRAINING WHEELS

Everyone has a script or a concept, which is more
than a script. No processing of ideas here it's all action,
every one a verb, super verb, reverberating in sound bites
up and down Queen Street. I am constantly walking
into walls, can't tell what is a door, closet. Brick is burnt
sienna watered down and sprayed at six paces. The secret
is in structure. (Hadn't we always suspected?)

UNION STATION

You don't move; hold your too-heavy bag, eyes fixed
on my right ear, two rocks, a stream, buzz of conversation,
spring. Do you recognize me without the layers? Without
the patois, harmonica, shrieking of taxi cabs and *(Maudite!)*
drunken undergrads? I'm the first to gesture, because I can.
Because I can see where I want us to go and you, I know,
have only your yearning. You say, *I don't trust you.* Your hand,
a curl, knapsack thumping to the floor. You say, *It may take
a long time.* I nod. I hope it does.

V

DOMESTIC BLISS

ON YOM KIPPUR

You fast with your family. In the marigold kitchen I push broccoli
around in circles. The cat stands at her bowl. She'll stand as long
as needed. It's only Saturday for me. Laundry folded, floors swept.
Shofar, torah, kippah, I am envious of what draws you — and the moon,
even the moon. At sundown I pour a glass of wine. Late,
your family drops you home, you bring me cake, but I want more.
It's a mistake to translate you say, not everything relates. While
you sleep, my old cat curled in the curve of your back, I trace
the line of your jaw, your lips,
searching.

YOUR HAIR

You put your hair up, take it down, put it up. I'm jealous
of the clips, elastics and fabrics, how you arrange, pat, admire.
Some days it's cotton candy: impossible to take just one strand,
and shiny, sweet smelling, finger-sticky — hopelesss to resist.
As a teenager your hair was thick and straight. You say it was
hormones. I imagine them uncontainable, springing. In a crowd
you are easy to spot. Look for hair. She has hair. When you rein it
in, strap it down, mournful, I sit on my hands. But there is no
restraining them, they know exactly what they want: to tickle
your cheek, caress your nose, lick your ear, beckon.

BEACONSFIELD AVENUE

If it's warm I sit at the window listening to drain-sparrows argue
over bits of feather and straw. In the chair that you found on Laval
and carried to Brunswick, now here, I close my eyes and every avenue
I've called home stretches before me, soft as my nine-year-old
Birkenstocks, warm as the cup of tea I hold. *And more to come*, you
say, *this is just the beginning.* In the hundred and twenty years since
its arrival in Brooklyn, the sparrow has established itself in every
North American city and town: Janis Joplin, Main Street, train station,
Disney. Close your eyes: wherever the car stops, the heel hits, the
hat lands lands, the heart rests, you're home. Even the cat, after
fifteen years of hunting, seems to appreciate the afternoon for its own
sake: she stretches her claws into the sun and listens.

ITALIAN LEATHER

This morning I tripped
over your square-toed boots,
and after cursing
held one like a seashell.

I could hear your footfalls,
on pavement, crunching
against the dry snows of Montréal,
slushing down Bloor Street, clicking
on a storm drain in London,
stumping through La Guardia,
Charles de Gaulle, Pearson.

I could hear your laugh bubbling,
cappuccino foam on your bottom lip,
shoulders undulating, and in the background
the honking of horns, *Basta! Basta!*
your tongue in my ear.

SONG FOR YOUR INSIDE OUT

Lips across the room, wings, arms
assume flight, the moon a lover I might
caress, planets I might come to know
the astronomy of your milky skin.
You fed me, stretched my appetite.
What was inside is now out.
What was out now discarded.
What was hard become supple.
Complications, distractions, playful, playful,
cat toy, cat nip, cat dancer, you are
my scratching post, I stretch into you, extend
the claws to the edge where the muscles contract, rakish
and proud when it comes to your body, when it comes
to my body, when it comes to our skin, when it comes
to fingers and the world, as you say, is juicy.

VI

FINCH & KEELE

1.

Behind us an oil depot: oversized white cakes, spiral staircases chain-
link-fenced. Grass trimmed. Trucks lined neatly. Under the power lines
a rapini farm, community gardens, parking meters: even this far north
of the lake parking is premium. Mornings I share the elevator
with women from Ghana, Somalia, Azerbaijan, Israel. They come
to practise English, see a doctor, look for work. Who knows why
we end up anywhere? In my windowless office I try to imagine
why a woman leaves a country where cyclamen grow wild, for traffic
jams, unswimmable bodies of water. *War is like smoke,* she says,
there's nowhere it does not slip in.

Some days my ignorance astounds.

2.

I work in six floors of mirror over a strip mall. False beacon,
it offers a checkerboard of sky, of clouds, of planes. It gives
nothing of itself. All winter long sparrows and starlings sing
out of cracks where retail signage is nestled over concrete pillars.
Toqued heads bow, pushing into the steamy lobby. The super
opens the door and smiles. It's just another building, on
another day, busy with velvet-slippered Canadians buying
donuts from Tim Horton's. Stuffed in the elevator this morning
the ground shifts, hungry blackbirds peck at the hem of my suit,
my fear palpable to small children who dart behind skirts, saris.
It isn't that I don't want to be here, it's that I'm not sure who
I am — twirl of tamarind and jasmine, patch of pink silk, of gold
earrings, brocaded satin scarves, so many scarves winding round
and round and round.

3.

Today I park outside the sex shop with its inflatable wide-eyed
blonde, a can of beer balanced on her hospitable head, smile
an inverted condom. Six boys from the Catholic school, ties
loosed, shirts untucked, smoke cigarettes and strike each other
like safety matches. Outside my building a man and woman flail
and yell, swing at each other and miss, swing again, and miss.
Two finches join in a fluttery spiral above them. People gather
at the doorway as the window washer glides his blade
across the glass.

4.

I drop my letter, let the chute fall with a clang, but the thunk
of metal does not stir the starling overhead, wings wide and flat
at her nest opening. Frozen. Preserved. A man leans against a pillar
beneath her. *But I do care,* he whispers into his cell phone, *I do,* eyes
on the back of a school girl who smokes, hums Celine Dion, a halo
of hair products and Juicy Fruit chewing gum. I want to turn,
but the stillness of the starling, the spike of her beak, hollow eyes,
and I wonder if her breast caught on a bit of metal; if there
are young inside, under her still wings, folded into each other
like translucent, nodding mushrooms. Or, if she had been
an aspiring bird who, in the face of spring and mating, spread
her wings for nothing more than the thrill of the dive.

5.

This morning I navigate Dufferin, past the Hooters drive-in, because
the police have blocked off my usual route for the usual reason. This
is a matter of bodies. Yellow tape across a road means violence, and
it's rarely that a woman has turned the blade on her attacker, ripped
the point in above the navel. So the bodies are usually female. These
are not necessary details. No relation to hooters or the Sunshine girl:
*Just a little something to make me smile, to break up the day, where's
the harm in that?* Even though we've all taken the same detour, heard
the same reports of the latest sixteen-year-old girl-body found
in a dumpster, we drink coffee, discuss insurance benefits, weekend
plans. It's only Tuesday. We're running out of new routes.

6.

Coke cans, condoms, Cheetos bags, falafel wrappers stiff against
the chain link fence separating wild grasses from the strip of parking
lot turf. Soon petunias will be planted in oval beds and, uncared for,
will wither. Meanwhile, nothing can contain the yellow hawkweed,
the lilac vetch that pushes through concrete. In May community
gardens sprout watering cans and seed bags, tomato plants, wheel-
barrows. Men and women in baseball caps and turbans, oblivious
to or accepting of traffic jams, airplanes, the transformer's hiss,
appear with rakes and trowels, their backs warm and bending
into summer.

VII

GIVING SHAPE TO GRIEF

If I separated myself from you,
I would turn entirely thorn.
— Rumi

1.

Can't keep up with illness. Bad news rings at all hours.
Yesterday I lost my sunglasses, drinking cup, pocket-sized

Sappho. It is the autumn of my mood. Shedding.
Axillary dissection. Oncologist. Tomoxaphen.

Everything about this new vocabulary slices. I want
to send you something whole and hopeful, to write

frivolity because there's still time for that. Something
about foxgloves, lilacs, familiar, fragrant. Things I love

at this moment: jagged peaks, pine trees, magpies, Erin,
Lisa, Angel, Norton Disk Doctor, paper. You.

2.

I can't sleep because I've not forgiven. Taut. Resentment
cements my lower back, anger tenses my neck. Over

and over your words knot my shoulders, even as my fingers
attempt to unravel. Touch my chest and I'll explode.

The world spins and beckons but I choose old, sad paths.
Why must I compare trailer parks with tin foil? Choices

startling as mushrooms in concrete; elephants on Spadina
Avenue. Do you forgive me? Or will I forgive myself?

3.

Starlings teach their young to fly from the grass up, not
nest down. You see, even good intentions can be murderous.

Daily I navigate the 401, merge and yield with seconds
to spare, yet I'm unable to reach you. I've seen the moon

up close. It is fluorescent, made of the same particles
as earth only in inverse proportion. What we lack she

has in abundance, and you? If I were brave
I would say I love you. Beg you to open. Loneliness

is like rust on hinges. On Mondays I believe in magic.
Mornings I wipe the slate and begin again. Never

stop up the keg. Pour and pour until we are so supple
we bend to the canvas, to the page, to the camera, in

this moment, and this, and this.

4.

When I'm afraid of solitude I know it's time to be alone.
Surrounded by chattering, muscles slacken. Discontent

is everywhere. Instead of experiencing the gray jays dancing
under lodgepoles I'm desperate to share this with you.

Listen. If suddenly you see a wing, listen.

Sometimes when I sing, I know I've not loved enough. I long
for prairie grass waving, a heart that huge. Can it be like that

for us? If eyes are the soul's window, feet are the heart's porthole.
Oil, eucalyptus, cream: the heel is where the poem is.

When I'm old I'll have a kayak, trace the coastline of
my beloved, follow a whale's song, become a rock

to rub on.

5.

She has moss in her hair, volcano mouth, ice receding
from the explosion of her heart; silt under nails, smell

of baked shark in the softest consonants. She conjugates verbs:
a need to conflate selected historiographies. Collage. Bruise

of memory. She arcs moonward, sorrow jet fuel, after burn
a trail of pastel flowers, and I know memory is not a template.

Sometimes love is too complicated for family. It's better spent
on hitchhikers or gardens full of beans and day lilies.

Maybe the trick is, knowing what kind of love you have,
what kind of wine to serve, how much of you

you are willing to offer with it.

6.

France, I've not seen your scar, only the fold in your shirt where
there was once flesh. Yet I feel it in my own breast, sudden and sharp.

I understand why you've let your hair grow. Celebrate and celebrate
the length of it. Let it go, grow luscious, wild. Uncontained.

My story of you has been so restrictive. Even my encouraging had
a shape for you to grow into. O but to love, just to love, as you are.

And I cannot look at knives now. Nor can I cut away a knot,
must undo and undo till my fingers numb, heart is aching, heavy.

What does a breast weigh? Do you feel it there still? Or dream it
somewhere frozen and erect. Lonely breasts, needing to be touched.

VIII

POSTCARDS
FROM
BANFF

MOROCCAN DINNER

Couscous expands to twice its size: eat it slowly with pine-
apple or red pepper; imagine Rumi whirling through snow.

Is it the heat, or must I eat only from your fingers? I want nothing
more than to dance, and it's the last thing I will let myself do.

The room is a sauna. Three Susans stand and a line forms.
Legs lift and kick, circling empty chairs and one forgotten cane.

Dulcimer, marimba, notes float and explode. I must have air. Elk
and mule deer sleep under pine trees. Shit everywhere.

Where are you tonight? The phone rings and rings, I haven't energy
to hang up, fall asleep to the possibility of you.

GRAPEFRUIT

This morning I rediscover the grapefruit: they smile up
from their iced platter. How soigné. Aunt Shirley

in her pink-tiled kitchen, tomato sauce already
simmering, rolling the fruit on the breadboard, slicing,

digging the edges, sugaring. Special knives, serrated,
doll-sized, plastic-handled: a rite of passage. Much later,

tart juice squeezed fresh into crystal: so much more
adult than the orange. Even now I feel a certain weight

as I dig my spoon into the fruit: ruby, glistening,
and even without sugar, I do not wince, dribble, or squint.

COMING BACK FROM TOWN

In the cemetery, two magpies disappear into a small mausoleum.
Snow has begun to stick. I lie flat on the path, expose my belly.

Flakes kiss and melt on my navel, tongue, closed eyes.
I remember you trailing a burst red balloon up Prince Arthur

in your wool coat, the harmonica lady paying no attention, smell
of wood smoke in your hair, snowploughs beeping and blinking.

Or, gin-drunk outside Café Sarajevo, how you wound yourself in
my silk, snow falling on your delicious, frosting neck. I long

to lick your lips, wipe your steamy little moons. Come to me now.
Slip your hand in my jeans. No one will find us here. Tell me

there's no way this cold can last.

OTHER MOUNTAINS

Sunset ascent, full moon hopeful. No need for rewrites here,
climb the trail, stand at the edge, don't imagine wings.

Uncle Baptiste with his walking stick, tossing rocks
onto German tents: *Le progrès, c'est pas bon, hein? Pas bon.*

Forgiveness arrives at the oddest moments. In the sound
of boots on gravel, wind on a mountain, tripping. Rock

is our blood. I stand on an outcrop, Bow River winding below,
recite my siblings' names, imagine a chiselled moment, each

of us frozen, each of us with our footpath. Black ice,
memory, absence. I stop and wave.

THE SECOND BLUE HOUR

5 am. Rock faces peer in my window. Not long ago, bison;
today me, sockless, sneezing. Someone is disappointed.

I want just a sliver of passion, a Victorian amount: coarseness
under table, china on top. Everything serviceable, elegant.

Ventriloquist at my window. Black caped. Too heavy for
the spruce tree tips, wing flutter, mountain-swallowing voice.

Plates shift under me. Spark of a spark to my sternum.
Feet lift, grip the mattress with my index fingers.

Soprano in my ear: bone china on rock. Release of wanting.
Release of expectation.

GIFTS

Once I believed poems were carved on skin. I presume
servitude still — but with less pain, more distance.

Empty glasses whirl and bang on beer-soaked tabletops.
Artists everywhere! More, more! Can't spin tales fast enough.

L., do you remember the night the tree fell, wedged
between two firs, an inch above our roof as you slept?

My father calls, tells me freedom is God's cruellest gift,
that he has hanged himself with it, is beyond redemption.

While we sleep, the elk and caribou laugh at the old
joke of us. Gifts aren't cruel, I tell us both, not accepting

them is. I dream him airborne, his taloned feet gigantic.

IX

THE NEXT TO LAST WINTER OF THE 20TH CENTURY

OR

THE ICE IS COOLER OVER THERE

HANUKKAH

Burgundy roses bloom in the balmy December morning,
newspapers over tea, elbows resting on the difficult stories.

Even if we read them, how can we express our horror?
The neighbour's guard dogs lift their legs against the security

signs and snap at each other. The lover of my imagination
is just like me, only smarter, wealthier, better looking,

in better shape, enlightened. Meanwhile, there is tea.
Meanwhile, what I cling to falls at my feet, my two cupped

hands overflow with shards of opportunity, impossible to grasp.
Can I fall in love with you once more? I check the five-pointed

star of our relationship and the tally is closer than the sun,
closer than the CN tower. The lover of my dreams lights

Hanukkah candles with her cashmere hands.

SUSHI ON QUEEN STREET

Sunday night. Eight women and between us we visit
Tel Aviv, Dublin, Cape Town, Joburg, Montreal, London,

Iceland, France, Guyana, Turkey, Prince George, Ottawa,
Grande Prairie, Saltspring and San Fransisco, all before

the main course. Millennial buzz is like pop rocks
on our tongues: laying in the supplies, the woodstoves,

oil lamps and dried fruit, just in case the technological
slipknot tightens. Safely we stoke our angst. We don't

really believe, but we're lesbians, our basements are filled
with food, champagne ordered months ago, we have

one eye on the back door, we know it can always
be kicked in. The sushi chef sails in a cargo boat filled

with fruit. It's December and the strawberries are fresh.

HIGH PARK

Each step rustles moths from the mulch of oak leaves.
Skaters circle artificial ice in T-shirts. Lou-dog whines

after a leaf fragment. At sixteen, my cat demands tuna, solid
tuna, and her own bed. The whole world is a little off.

At the Price Chopper I read about a ten year old beaten
for a gym bag, and the rape of Kosovar women. Neither fact

surprises. We have war, we have tea, we have pets
with better health care, better diets, than whole villages.

I chide myself for calculating the hidden costs of everything.
I tell the cashier she has beautiful hair. I recycle all

my plastic bags.

ANGRY

If we doubted winter's power, now we're on our knees.
Cars frozen over, snow piles layered, hardening, roads

reduced to one lane, nowhere to park. We have storms
inside too, and a crack in the foundation.

I shovel the walk, and daily it is buried. I want
to clear a path back to you, want to move the layers of

unspoken suffocating, want to lay my head on your chest,
want to feed you sip by sip, red wine lip to lip. Angry,

you paint your room pink, hang flowered curtains, drink
crantinis, smoke cigarettes, make dates away. Can't you see

how I ache: my gnawed fingers, my rice cake diet? We
find ourselves on the corner of Havelock and College: eye

to eye, hands hanging numb. Empty, you turn away again.

NASTURTIUM

Some mornings my heart is a lemon wedge. Other mornings
a nasturtium. Others a block of ice. Today an empty bottle of merlot.

Once I planted beans and sunflowers sprouted. Stalks so huge
I gathered scissors, rock, hammer: it's important to be prepared.

For years I've carried a pain in my ribs. Last night a child
with crocus fingers touched me there and a harmony of moths

flew up. My turn to ascend: the rungs cold, ridges cut the soles.
Aurelia aurita below: moon jelly, disk-shaped, fringed.

Through a microscope, even mundane emotions obscure.
Do you feel as rebellious as I? Will you leap?

CHEMICAL

At thirty-five it occurs to me I will not become
someone else. To celebrate, I take up meditation;

out of fear, I buy a gym pass. Both decisions provide
endless hours of guilt. Contentedness induces misery.

There's nowhere else I'd rather be than anywhere but here.
Here, now, I yearn for where I once wasn't. That's the struggle.

L. says it's chemical, this need to make decisions over
and over. How to progress covering the same ground

twenty different ways? And why must intention be rooted
out, be pure? The truest intention is transformed by

a spring breeze, or the scent of hyacinth. This is who
I am right now: tummy softening, hair like a pubescent

boy, fear of interest rates, love of the edge, longing
for a cushioned fall.

BARREN

I dreamed myself adrift. Fridtjof Nansen rescued me.
He said nothing. A fire burned in the belly of his ship.

Who knows where he found wood. Who knows how I landed
in a rowboat. Who knows how long I paddled before realizing

I was lost. Who knows how we survive anything. Some
people journey across oceans, strap food on their backs,

ride donkeys, camels, cutters, set off into barren landscapes.
Others close their eyes and journey in a heartbeat. Others

wrap themselves in wool and walk to the streetcar. There
are those who swallow pills. Some days lifting the blanket

is a chore. There's a sound an abandoned heart makes, so sharp
it has been known to cut through ice. Some days

the whole world vibrates with it.

SNOWSHOEING

Up and down Bloor Street shops close early. Tentative, we slip
into mukluks, strap on Gillian's snowshoes. Crystal air, sharp

in the lungs and mute, we navigate the high banks, looking down
into Christmas lit windows, all muffled and snug.

In Dufferin Park we sink to our knees — but it's a thrill to feel
the toes, the soles of the feet protected only by a thin strip

of leather. We fall flat, run, fall flat. In the playground
Quebecois children hang upside down, their laugh tropical, as if

the park is a sandy beach, the drifts, dunes, and at any moment:
song of the ice cream truck.

CROCUS

All day I wander around upsetting the houseplants.
Clouds press down on us like cotton wool in a pill jar.

Not even poetry can replace the first crocus
and if more people were concerned with crocuses —

well then. We drink to the resurrected heart barely rhyming
after the long, cold, corporate winter, the heating bills

and taxes, rejection letters piled next to the kitty litter.
I'm telling you there's nothing of substance here!

Your time is better spent counting the blossoms
on your block, the types of pests in your garden, the number

of ants you have stepped on, birds you've not seen, smiles
unnoticed. There is nothing I can say here to ease you.

I can't even ease me.

ICEBERGS

I clear my desk, lay a runner down, set a white bowl
in the center, frozen rose, still sweet, on the silk,

place an ice cube in the bowl, light a white candle and prepare
to leave much behind. When I close my eyes, narwhals

break through the polar cap, and Amma, raven-haired, jumps
from floe to floe, water-filled gumboots sloshing, waving me on

with the same determination she reserved for solitaire. She tells me
she's okay with how I've used her name. She's even created

her own word for lesbian, but in Icelandic, not English. Icebergs
are my ancestors. This family given to long nights of alcohol

and singing, table-dancing, waiting for the sun to come up.
Don't worry about us, she says. *We're in for the long haul.*

Even now, I can smell the ice cube melting.

THANKS & ACKNOWLEDGEMENTS

The list of books and authors that have inspired this work might be longer than the work itself. With that in mind I'd like to acknowledge a great debt to a small sampling of authors whose work has helped shape these poems: Dionne Brand, Daphne Marlatt, Michael Ondaatje, Phyllis Webb, John Thompson, Robert Kroetsch, Mary Oliver, Walt Whitman, Allen Ginsberg, the translations of Rumi by Coleman Barks, translations of Sappho by Mary Barnard, translations of Pablo Neruda by Stephen Mitchell. "Song for your inside out" was inspired by Sharon Olds' poem "Sex without love" which appeared in *The Dead and The Living* (Knopf 1983). "Scrabbling" is, in part, a response to Marilyn Hacker's book *Love, Death and the Changing of the Seasons* (Norton 1986).

Earlier versions of some of these poems have appeared in journals, including: *The Malahat Review, Pottersfield Portfolio,* and *Prairie Fire* as well as *Rip Rap: Fiction and Poetry from the Banff Centre for the Arts, The Poetry Page* (www.greenboathouse.com) and as a Broadside from Greenboathouse Books. To all the editors, a big thanks.

I'd especially like to thank The Banff Centre for the Arts where this work was both conceived and realized. Thanks to Rachel Wyatt, Edna Alford, Tim Lilburn, Daphne Marlatt, Don McKay, and in particular, the participants of the 1997 Writing Studio for raising the bar.

Thanks are also due to the Toronto Arts Council, The Canada Council, and Ontario Arts Council for essential writing time.

I am grateful to Kate Johnston, Margaret Webb, and Jennifer Duncan for ongoing reading and support. Ron Smith, thank you. Big hugs to Chris Willcox for "Sinking." Thank you to Michael Holmes and ECW. Thanks also to Chris Plunkett, Sylvia Hunt, Martha Hillhouse, Nick Lockson, Karen Grant, Theresa Stowe, Luce Roberts, Ferron, and to my family — especially my sister France, who continues to inspire.

Danielle — you make it possible.